DEALING WITH...
SCREEN TIME
Mitchell Lane
PUBLISHERS
KELLI HICKS

Parent and Caregiver Tips for Creating Nonfiction Readers

Timely topics in the *Dealing With...* series will interest intermediate and middle school readers and equip them with helpful strategies for coping with difficult situations. Your reader will be introduced to new concepts, facts, ideas, and vocabulary.

Tips for Reading Nonfiction

Talk about Nonfiction

Explain that nonfiction books provide facts about real-world topics. When readers read nonfiction, they gain a rich understanding of the world. They build background knowledge that provides a foundation for learning and academic success.

Look at the Parts

This book contains the following helpful features. Share the purpose of each feature with your reader.

Photos, Captions, and Graphic Aids

The photos, captions, charts, and other graphic aids in nonfiction texts contain a wealth of information. Help your reader identify different ways information can be displayed.

Sidebars

These extra tidbits of information help satisfy readers' curiosity and expand their knowledge.

Table of Contents

Located at the front of the book, this list shows the big ideas within the text and the page numbers where they can be found.

Extension Activities and Additional Resources

A "Your Turn" quiz and "Exploration and Discovery" activities invite readers to apply their new knowledge. Supporting resources are provided in a special "You Are Not Alone" section.

Glossary

Located at the back of the book, the glossary defines key words and phrases that are related to the topic. These words and phrases can be found in the text in **bold** type.

Index

Located at the back of the book, the index is an alphabetical list of topics and the page numbers where they can be found.

With a little help and guidance, your reader will be on their way to enjoying and learning from nonfiction books.

Mitchell Lane

PUBLISHERS

mitchelllanepub.com

2001 SW 31st Avenue
Hallandale, FL 33009

First Edition, 2026.
Author: Kelli Hicks
Designer: Rhea Magaro
Editor: Kim Thompson

Series: Dealing With...
Title: Dealing with Screen Time / by Kelli Hicks

Hallandale, FL : Mitchell Lane Publishers, [2026]

Library bound ISBN: 979-8-89260-675-2
eBook ISBN: 979-8-89260-678-3

PHOTO CREDITS
Shutterstock: Ground Picture, cover, 1, 27; ARVD73, 5; Prostock-studio, 6, 11, 17; Pixel-Shot, 7, 47; metamorworks, 9; Motortion Films, 10; Gorodenkoff, 12, 14, 15; Nuchylee, 13; smolaw, 16; fizkes, 18; Lapina, 19; Rido, 20; Peter Snaterse, 21; Nizwa Design, 22; nimito, 23; Ninja SS, 24; Gladskikh Tatiana, 25; Towfiqu ahamed barbhuiya, 28; Javvan, 29; Fabio Principe, 30; Tada Images, 32; PeopleImages.com - Yuri A, 33; Mike Orlov, 34; Daisy Daisy, 35; Madhourse, 36; 2xSamara.com, 37; casejustin, 37; Alive Color Stock, 38; Christos Georghiou, 39; Yulia Smir, 40; Fotokostic, 41; iofoto, 42; YasnaTen, 43; Shakirov Albert 44

Table of Contents

Chapter 1: Game On!

Elijah

Elijah runs his fingers through his hair. *When was the last time I took a shower?* he thinks. He quickly dismisses the thought and gets back to his game. He stayed up late watching YouTube videos with tips for getting hit points. He wants to try out the ideas before he has to leave for school. There won't be time to brush his teeth or eat breakfast. No big deal. He'll just grab a donut on the way out the door. Hopefully, he won't miss the bus like he has a few times before.

Just then, his character finds a passageway to a new dungeon. "Sweet!" Elijah exclaims.

After school, Elijah throws down his backpack and grabs a bag of chips. His mom is headed out. "I have to run to the store," she says. "Get started on your homework before I get back, okay?"

Elijah nods and heads to the other room. He gets online to keep playing his game.

It seems like only a minute has passed when Elijah hears his mom. "Earth to Elijah," she calls. "I said, is your homework done?"

Elijah is **agitated**. Doesn't she know that a mob of zombies is after his character? His heart beats fast. He tells a lie so he can keep playing. "Geez, Mom, leave me alone. It's done, alright?"

What Do You Think?

- What decisions does Elijah make? What consequences do his decisions have?
- What emotions does Elijah experience at different points in the story?
- Elijah spends all of his non-school hours online. How much of your day do you spend interacting with screens?
- Elijah is completely focused on screen time. Have you ever felt like Elijah?

Elijah feels bad about lying. He knows there's a list of missing assignments in his backpack that he needs to finish. If he doesn't, he'll fail math and English for this grading period. He's embarrassed. His mom is going to find out. Elijah is so mad at himself. But he still really wants to get back to his game.

Chapter 2: What Is Screen Time?

Do you watch funny videos on YouTube? Play online games? Video chat with your grandparents? Post on social media and check to see who likes your posts?

If you said yes, you know all about screen time. Screens are all around you. They're on smartphones, tablets, smartwatches, computers, and TVs. They let you access a world of information 24 hours a day, seven days a week. Screen time is the total amount of time you spend looking at and interacting with these devices.

There are many benefits to digital **content**. How else would you work on a research project or find out about world events? Screens provide learning games to help you in school. They connect you to family and friends. They can show you how to improve your soccer skills, knit a scarf, or do the latest dance.

Did You Know?

Too much screen time can harm your eyes. It can cause a condition called asthenopia. Symptoms include headaches, dry eyes, eye pain, and fatigue.

Unfortunately, too much screen time can create problems. It can interfere with other important parts of your life. It can interrupt your sleep, alter your mood, and even prevent your brain from working at its best.

Types of Screen Time

There are different types of screen time. Each affects your mind and body in different ways.

Passive Screen Time

Passive screen time happens when you sit still in front of a screen without moving or interacting with others. Your body and mind are **idle** as you binge-watch episodes of a TV show, look at TikTok videos on a tablet, or scroll through other people's social media posts on your phone.

Active Screen Time

Active screen time requires you to think or move. When you play a video game, your mind and body are **engaged** as you make choices and work the controller. Using technology to create music, videos, or artwork is another example of active screen time. Doing educational activities on a screen, such as researching or completing homework, also falls into this category.

Social Screen Time

Social screen time happens when you use digital tools to reach out to others and talk to them. Screens help you stay in touch with friends and family members. This type of screen time includes texting and video conferencing. It also includes making social media posts or commenting on other people's posts.

Screen Time and the Brain

Researchers wondered if screen time impacts the brain, especially the brains of young people. They ran studies to learn about the developing brain and technology use. They found out that, yes, technology does affect the way kids' brains work.

Studies Show That Too Much Screen Time Can...

- Affect how you observe and experience activities in real life.
- Change how you learn about and participate in the world.
- Limit your mental, social, and emotional development.

Researchers found a **correlation** between large amounts of screen time and reduced communication skills. They discovered that kids who spend a lot of time with screens have fewer problem-solving skills.

The National Institutes of Health (NIH) conducted a study on kids with more than two hours of daily screen time. The researchers compared them to kids with less than two hours of daily screen time. They found that the young people who spent more time on screens scored lower on language and thinking tests.

There Is Good News!

When used in moderation and with adult support, playing video games and exploring educational digital content can increase problem-solving skills and improve flexible thinking.

The same study reached another conclusion about kids who use screens for more than seven hours each day. Scans showed that an **excessive** amount of screen time was related to thinning of the brain's cortex. The cortex is the part of the brain responsible for critical thinking and reasoning.

Engaging in screen time often makes you feel good. Video games have fun challenges and rewards. TV shows and videos make you laugh. Getting a like on your social media post fills you with pride.

When an activity **stimulates** you and makes you happy, a chemical called **dopamine** gets released in your brain. Dopamine is important for health. It helps you focus and remember. It makes you feel motivated.

But when dopamine gets released too often, negative effects can happen. Your brain gets used to having lots of dopamine all the time. You feel a constant need to keep doing stimulating activities. Since screens are all around you, you reach for them again and again. You may develop a **behavioral addiction** to screen time.

This type of addiction can make you choose screens over things that are less fun but that have more long-term rewards, such as schoolwork, chores, or exercise. Over time, this will have negative effects on your mood and your life.

Screen Time and Individual Differences

Some people are more likely to spend too much time on screens than others. Kids who are less busy with friends and extracurricular activities have more time for screens. Kids who struggle with **anxiety** may find it easier to interact with a screen than with real people and situations. Kids who have ADHD may prefer reading short social media posts instead of longer books.

In these cases, using screens can become a negative cycle. As people spend more time on screens, their issues get worse. As their issues get worse, they spend more time on screens.

Did You Know?

People experiencing **depression**, anxiety, or ADHD are more likely to use screens as a way to isolate themselves and avoid challenging situations.

Chapter 3: The Risks of Screen Time

There are many risks involved with spending too many hours of the day on screens. Here are some to watch out for.

School-Related Risks

Too much screen time can limit the development of your vocabulary and language skills. It can take the place of reading books. It can make it harder to concentrate on schoolwork. All these factors can lead to lower grades and test scores.

If you spend all your time online, you are less likely to get involved in clubs, sports, and other after-school activities. You miss out on making healthy connections with teachers, coaches, and other students.

Social Risks

If you are always online, you miss out on seeing friends and family members in real life. Your imagination doesn't get a workout coming up with new ways to have fun, be creative, and relax.

Looking at other people's social media posts can make you think you're missing out on all the fun. You may feel like you don't really know your friends and they don't really know you.

Physical Health Risks

It's not good to sit for too long without moving your body. People who spend hours each day passively watching screens are more likely to be overweight. This can lead to issues with body image and low **self-esteem**.

Growing bodies need sleep to recharge. At night, your body produces a **hormone** called melatonin that helps you sleep. Digital devices emit a blue light that **suppresses** melatonin. Using these devices after dark keeps you awake and alert even when you need to sleep.

Mental Health Risks

Kids who overuse digital devices may have poor social skills. This can lead to loneliness and isolation. Comparing your own life to the "perfect" lives that people try to show on their social media accounts can lower your self-esteem. It can lead to anxiety and depression.

Kids who spend too much time online can be exposed to content that is mature, violent, or inappropriate. They may become **desensitized** to the images they see.

Studies Show That...

- Kids spend twice as much time playing on screens as they do playing outside.
- Three out of four kids don't get enough physical activity.
- One in four kids believes that playing video games counts as exercise.

When Is Screen Time a Problem?

How do you know if screen time is a problem for you? Ask yourself these questions.

- ☐ Do I rarely spend time with friends in real life?
- ☐ Do I find it hard to listen to someone and focus during an in-person conversation?
- ☐ Do I avoid in-person activities or isolate myself from family and friends in order to have screen time?
- ☐ Does being on screens seem to take up all my free time and energy?
- ☐ Does screen time interfere with getting my homework done?
- ☐ Do I think about online activities even when I'm not online?
- ☐ Does screen time interfere with my desire to go to school, with my focus in class, or with my ability to complete assignments?
- ☐ Do my online activities make me feel bad about myself?
- ☐ Do my online activities make me feel frustrated or lead to angry outbursts?

If you answered yes to any of these questions, it is time to evaluate your screen time and make some changes. Don't worry! The next chapter is full of helpful ideas.

Chapter 4: Strategies for Taking Control

Are you spending too much of your daily life on screens? Don't worry! There are many strategies that will help you take control of your screen time and feel healthier and happier.

Strategy #1: Create Screen-Free Zones

Create device-free zones in your home to help you concentrate, connect with others, and get things done. Except for educational tools you need, your homework space should be free of digital devices. Other screen-free zones might be the breakfast or dinner table, a space for creating art or doing a hobby, or your backyard. Talk with your family about gathering devices in one room so you can enjoy screen time together.

Zones can also be times of the day. Having a screen-free hour after school can help you relax. Putting devices away during certain times will make it easier to exercise, spend time with family members, and do chores.

There IS Good News!

Many internet browsers and social media platforms have controls you and your parents can set to limit the amount of sensitive or inappropriate content you see. These settings can make you healthier and safer. Explore your options with a trusted adult.

Strategy #2: Find an Accountability Partner

Ask a friend or adult you trust to be your screen-time **accountability** partner. Explain your goals to them and ask them to help you keep your promise to be screen-free at certain times or in certain situations. You and your partner can challenge each other to be more active, join a team or club, and share your success.

Identify an adult you trust to be your accountability partner for digital content. Seek their advice when you see content that raises questions or makes you uncomfortable in any way. Ask them to help you establish guidelines for online searches and select settings on your devices that will keep you safe.

Strategy #3: Track Your Screen Time

Look for patterns in the way you use technology. Are you scrolling while waiting for the bus or when you are bored? Do you start doing your homework and end up watching videos? When you see how your time is being spent, you can set helpful limits.

You don't need to give up all your time online. You can reduce it a little bit at a time. Block apps that cause you **distractions** and turn off notifications. Some social media platforms have built-in time-tracking tools. They can help you understand how much time you spend online and set a goal to cut back. There are also apps such as ScreenZen and AntiSocial that can help you monitor and manage screen time.

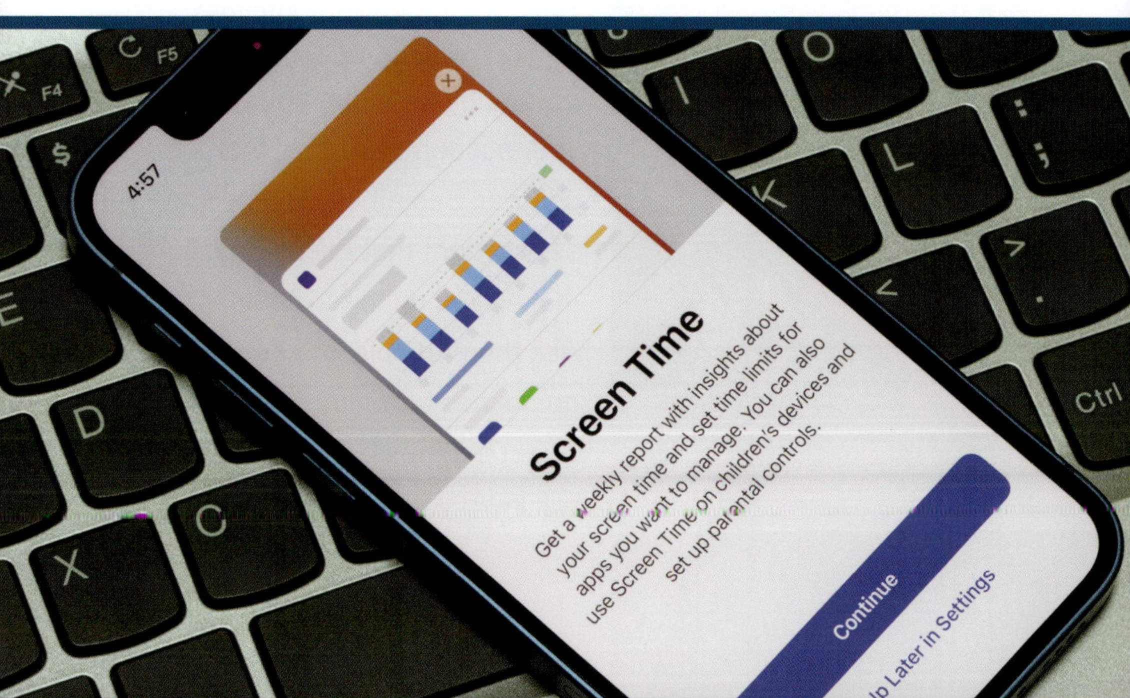

Did You Know?

The American Academy of Pediatrics (AAP) and the World Health Organization (WHO) developed guidelines for screen time based on age.

- Ages less than 1: No screen time
- Ages 1 to 2: No screen time except video chatting with family members and limited viewing with a parent
- Ages 2 to 5: No more than one hour daily of viewing high-quality programming with a parent or sibling
- Ages 5 to 17: No more than two hours daily, except to complete schoolwork

Strategy #4: Get Moving and Doing

Replace screen time with physical activity. Find fun ways to get your body moving. Set up time to meet friends in person for riding bikes or playing a sport. Don't be afraid to try something new. Have you always wanted to play volleyball or tennis? Do it! Look for opportunities in your community.

There IS Good News!

You can form a new habit in about 60 days. To build good habits, associate healthy behaviors with things that reward you and make you feel good. For example, you can listen to music you enjoy while exercising.

Creating things with your hands is a fun and relaxing break from screen time. Try painting or crochet. Spend time making a model or building a collection. Being more active in the real world will give you a sense of accomplishment and make you feel great.

Strategy #5: Avoid Screens at Bedtime

Your body needs quality sleep to recharge for the next day. Getting enough sleep helps you focus, make good decisions, and stay in a good mood.

You can make your bedroom a screen-free zone. Or you can plan to shut down screens during your nighttime routine. Turn off devices and remove them from your bedroom one hour before you go to bed. This will reduce blue light and help you relax. Your parents and other family members can help you stick to healthy sleep habits.

Studies Show That...

Most students do not get enough sleep. Here are recommended guidelines from the CDC (Centers for Disease Control).

- Kids ages 6 to 12 need 9 to 12 hours of sleep each night.
- Teens ages 13 to 18 need 8 to 10 hours of sleep each night.

Strategy #6: Use Screens Mindfully

When you use a digital device, ask yourself why. Do you have a good reason? Are you bored? Are you avoiding other things? Take steps to cut out screen time that is without purpose or that might not be positive.

Practicing **mindfulness** helps you get in touch with your thoughts, feelings, and needs. It helps you focus on what is happening in the present. Take a moment to slow down and calmly look around. What real things can you see, hear, and touch? Notice details. Take slow, deep breaths. Then, check in with yourself. What is best for you at this moment?

There IS Good News!

Learning to be more mindful helps to develop your brain's cortex. It can reverse the effects of too much screen time.

Chapter 5: Dealing with Screen Time

Remember Elijah? A few days later, his math teacher called and let his mom know that Elijah had missed many assignments. Elijah did not try to deny it. He was almost relieved. His mom asked how she could help Elijah get back on track.

Elijah admitted he was spending too much time and energy on video games. It was starting to negatively affect his life. He felt embarrassed, but he wasn't sure what to do about it.

Elijah and his mom decided to make their kitchen a screen-free zone. Elijah would do homework at the kitchen table while his mom

fixed dinner. The two could talk, and Elijah's mom could help keep him accountable. Elijah would still have time to play video games for a short time after school and after his homework was complete. But all screens would be turned off at eight o'clock so Elijah could have a relaxing shower before bed.

Elijah mentioned he would like to try out for the school soccer team. His mom reminded him that kids met up to play soccer at the park on Saturdays. Elijah decided to join them that weekend.

Elijah felt better knowing he had people to support him. He knew it would be hard to limit his screen time, but he was ready to make a positive change.

Remember: You can take control of screen time so that it doesn't control you!

YOUR TURN: HOW DO YOU DEAL WITH SCREEN TIME?

For each situation, select the answer most likely to produce the best outcome. Make a note of your answers on a separate sheet of paper.

1. Jasmine spends an average of six hours a day on her phone, mostly scrolling through her social media accounts. She has noticed she feels more anxious and less focused at school. What could she do to control her anxiety?
   - **A.** Continue using her phone for the same amount of time, but go down to only one social media platform.
   - **B.** Schedule phone-free times each day.
   - **C.** Ask her friends to join her for more online activities and games.

2. Julio's parents are concerned because he plays video games for about nine hours each day on the weekends. They notice he often feels tired during the week. What is a good first step for Julio's parents to take?
   - **A.** Take away all Julio's electronic devices for a month.
   - **B.** Encourage Julio to play games only during the week.
   - **C.** Help Julio set a limit for his weekend gaming hours.

3. Keira loves binge-watching TV shows, but she realizes she is not getting her homework done. She has a big project due soon, but she feels overwhelmed. What could help Keira manage her time?
   - **A.** Finish all episodes of her latest show and then start her project.
   - **B.** Create a schedule for working on her project first and watching TV as a reward. Ask her sister to help keep her accountable.
   - **C.** Promise herself that she won't watch TV or do any other activities until the project is done.

4. Tony loves to watch videos online, but he has started to experience headaches and eye strain. He often forgets to take breaks. What should Tony do?
   - **A.** Use an app to remind him to take breaks every 20 minutes.
   - **B.** Increase the brightness of his screen.
   - **C.** Switch to watching longer videos so that he feels more engaged.

Think about your answers.

1. The best answer is B. Jasmine can reduce her anxiety and improve her focus by taking breaks from her screen.
2. The best answer is C. Julio needs to reduce his weekend screen time. That way, he'll have time to rest and recover from the previous week and get ready for the next week.
3. The best answer is B. Keira needs a strategy to find balance. She will be more successful if she sticks to a schedule with her sister's help.
4. The best answer is A. Frequent breaks will reduce Tony's eye strain and help him feel better. Getting up to take a walk or do some other physical activity will help him feel better overall.

Exploration and Discovery: Activities to Try

1. Think about all the hobbies and activities you have always wanted to try. Create a poster that shows your ideas. Replace some of your screen time with the activities on your list. See how many you can check off.
2. Develop a screen time plan. Include time when you need to be online for schoolwork. Think about how you can make your other time on devices more active than passive. Build in rewards for reducing your weekly screen time.
3. For one week, track how much time you spend online and how you feel. Is there a relationship between your screen time and your emotions?
4. Talk to a group of friends about excessive screen time. Make plans to meet up frequently for real-life activities such as pick-up sports games, taking hikes, or completing creative projects.

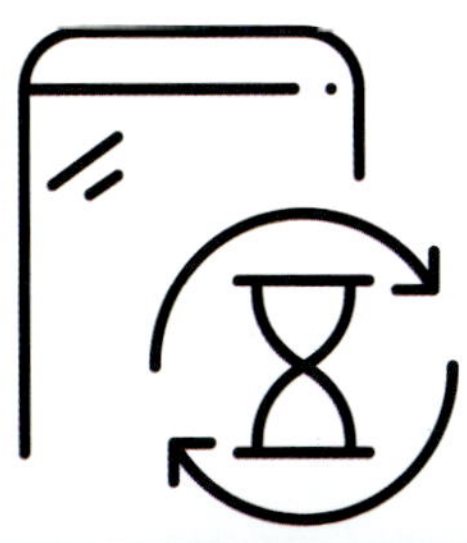

YOU ARE NOT ALONE

Dealing with screen time can make you feel exhausted and alone. But you are NOT alone. There are good people who care about you and want to help. There are also many resources you can use to learn more and help yourself.

Explore some of these ways to find the kindness and support you deserve.

People to Ask for Help

- ☑ guidance counselor
- ☑ teacher
- ☑ principal
- ☑ assistant principal
- ☑ parent
- ☑ older sibling
- ☑ grandparent
- ☑ aunt or uncle
- ☑ coach
- ☑ school secretary
- ☑ bus driver
- ☑ religious youth group leader
- ☑ any friend that you trust
- ☑ any adult that you trust

Websites

BBC: My Teenage Brain: Why Can't I Stop Scrolling?
www.bbc.co.uk/bitesize/articles/zt99mbk#zn77s82
Learn about the relationship between screen time and dopamine and find healthy solutions.

Learn Free: Why We Can't Stop Scrolling
www.youtube.com/watch?v=uBkeKv_6U4c
This video explains how screen time can lead to behavioral addiction.

Nemours KidsHealth: Online Safety
kidshealth.org/en/kids/online-id.html
Learn important rules to follow for staying safe online.

Books

Bocci, Goali Saedi. *The Social Media Workbook for Teens: Skills to Help You Balance Screen Time, Manage Stress, and Take Charge of Your Life*. New Harbinger Publications Inc., 2019.

Brian, Rachel. *(Be Smart About) Screen Time!: Stay Grounded, Set Boundaries, and Keep Safe Online*. Little, Brown Books for Young Readers, 2024.

Morris, Taylor. *You're Addicted to Your Phone: How to Break the Habit (Social Media Smarts)*. Enslow Publishing, 2019.

Phone Helplines

Crisis Text Line
Text HOME to 741741 or message on WhatsApp. Young people of color can text STEVE to 741741 to reach culturally trained counselors.

LGBT National Youth Talkline
1-800-246-7743

National Suicide Prevention Lifeline
1-800-273-8255

Suicide and Crisis Lifeline
Call or text 988.

GLOSSARY

accountability (uh-koun-tuh-BI-luh-tee)
Willingness to accept responsibility for your actions

agitated (AJ-i-tay-tid)
Nervous or upset; shaken up

anxiety (ang-ZYE-i-tee)
Feelings of worry or fear

behavioral addiction (bi-HAY-vyuh-ruhl uh-DIK-shuhn)
A compulsive or chronic need to do something or take certain actions; strongly inclined to indulge in something over and over

content (KAHN-tent)
The words, photos, music, and other matter that appears on a website or digital platform

correlation (kor-uh-LAY-shuhn)
A relationship discovered between things

depression (di-PRESH-uhn)
Unhappiness that doesn't go away

desensitized (dee-SEN-suh-tized)
Used to something, not sensitive, or not caring

distractions (di-STRAKT-shuhnz)
Things that take your focus away from what you are doing or what you need to do

dopamine (DOH-puh-meen)
A hormone in the brain that governs attention, memory, and mood

engaged (en-GAYJD)
Busy and focused on doing something

excessive (ik-SES-iv)
More than necessary; too much

hormone (HOR-mone)
A chemical made by the body that affects growth, development, and behavior

idle (EYE-duhl)
Not busy; lazy

mindfulness (MINDE-fuhl-nis)
The practice of focusing your attention on the present moment

self-esteem (self i-STEEM)
How someone thinks about themself and their capabilities

stimulates (STIM-yuh-lates)
Causes interest and excitement by engaging your senses

suppresses (suh-PRES-is)
Holds back or puts a stop to something

INDEX

ABOUT THE AUTHOR

Kelli Hicks is a teacher, mom, and author who lives in Tampa, Florida. She tries her best to help her students and her own kids deal with screen time. It is a difficult balance, but she knows how important it is to take breaks and work on being a well-rounded human. Kelli makes sure to exercise and take social media breaks to deal with the pressures and demands of screen time.